Handmade Jewelry.

Everything You Need To Know To Begin Making Handmade Beaded Jewelry.

Table Of Contents

Copyright

Introduction

I want to thank you and congratulate you for downloading the book, *"Handmade Jewelry: Everything You Need To Know To Begin Making Handmade Beaded Jewelry."*

This book contains everything you need to know to begin making beautiful handmade jewelry.

(In this book you are going to learn how to make several different types of jewelry. I will walk you through the steps you need to take in order to create each project and make it your very own. In this book you will learn how to make beautiful projects such as hair pins, necklaces, bracelets, earrings and much more. For each of these projects you will need a few basic items but what you will need the most of while working through this book is a variety of beads. You are also going to learn tons of beading tips and tricks in this book as I have tried to incorporate them in to each chapter. When you finish reading the book not only will you have created amazing handmade jewelry projects but you will be ready to get creative and make projects of your own. I hope you enjoy reading this book and working through the projects! Watch out at the end of this book for my special bonus, how to create your very own beads out of newspaper or any other type of paper you would like to recycle!)

Thanks again for downloading this book, I hope you enjoy it!

Chapter 1
Creating a beautiful jeweled hair pin or comb and more!

We are going to start with a very simple project, it is the basic beaded bobby pin. In order to create this you will need a few simple materials that include: of course a bobby pin, some wire (20 gauge will work great for this project), scissors, and a ruler, and an assortment of beads. Seed beads are great for this project but you can use any bead you would like.

Now it is time to get started creating your beaded bobby pin. The first thing you want to do is to cut your wire to 18 inches. Now you can put your roll of wire, scissors, and ruler to the side, you will not need these for now.

Now you need to hole the bobby pin with the loop pointing up and the straight side facing you. Now you are going to take the center of the wire and wrap it around the straight side of the bobby pin holding it secure. Next you will take the right end of the wire and stick it through the bobby pin so that it goes to the left side. Wrap the same piece over the bobby pin to the right side so that it is back on the right side again.

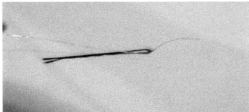

Now you are going to do the same thing with your left strand except you are going to go the opposite way. Take the left end of your wire and push it through the bobby pin so that it is on the right side of the pin, then wrap it back over the pin so that the wire is back on the left side of the pin.

You will be able to push the wire to the top of the straight side of the bobby pin at this point just make sure you do not push it too far up where it is in the loop.

It is time to start adding your beads now so you can pick out the first bead that you want to add to your bobby pin. Bringing both of the strands of wire together you are going to thread your bead through both of them at the same time. If the ends are uneven it is okay at this point to trim a little off of the wire in order to make them even and make threading the bead easier.

Once you have your bead threaded on the wire you want to push it all the way up to the bobby pin. After you have pushed to bead all the way up to the top of the bobby pin you need to separate your wires and do just as you did when you were securing the wire in the first place.

Take the left wire and go into the bobby pin until it is on the right side, and then wrap it back over to the left side. Take the right wire and go into the bobby pin until it is on the left side, and then wrap it back over to the right side. Make sure that your bead is snug and secure on the bobby pin.

Bring your wires back together and thread your next bead. You will continue to do this until you have the design that you want on your bobby pin. Once you have finished beading your bobby pin you will take each side of your wire and wrap them around the end three times, you should not do both wires at the same time. For example you will take the left wire and wrap it three times then take the right wire and wrap it three times. Make sure that you do not wrap both of the ends of the bobby pin together when you are doing this.

Once you have wrapped each of the sides of the wire three times the only thing that is left to do is snip of the left over ends of the wire and tuck the wire in so that it does not poke you when you are wearing the bobby pin.

When you are making this project you can create thousands o different beaded bobby pins, you can used different colored bobby pins as well as different colored wire. The possibilities are endless and you can let your imagination run wild. One grea thing that you can do with this is match the colors to you outfits. So if you really like your pink shirt you can create a bobby pin that will match it.

For the next project I want to teach you how to create beautif beaded hair combs. These are great for brides, or just every da wear. Just like the beaded bobby pins you can also make this match your outfits.

You can use any bead that you want when you are creating beaded hair comb from seed beads to crystals and even pearls is completely up to you and all depends on what you want create. I am including this project because it is another ve simple project to help you get started creating beautiful jewelry

Of course you will need a hair comb to complete this proje there are some that have loops in the back that are made just f projects like this but you can also use a regular hair comb. F this project I am going to discuss how to make a beaded h comb using the comb with the loops.

In addition to the hair combs you will need some super NEW glue, illusion cord, wire cutters, or scissors and your beads.

The illusion cord is very thin and it is a little hard to see so you will not be able to see it once your project is finished. You will want to start out with about 2 feet of cord. To start making your hair comb you will put the cord through the first loop of your comb and just make a simple knot securing it to the comb. The back of your comb will be where your knot is.

Now take the end of your cording and slip it through the first loop of the comb, you will want to go through the back of your comb and bring it out the front of your comb. Now you can add your first bead. Once you have your first bead on it is up to you if you want to continue to add beads or just create a very simple comb going straight down the line.

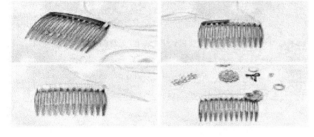

For this project we are just going to create a simple comb so what you will need to do after you add the first bead is push your cording through the second hole by going in the front and coming out of the back of the comb, then thread the cording through the back of the third hole and come out the front of it. It will look a little bit like sewing while you are doing this. Add your next bead and since your cording is coming out of hole number three, go into hole number four, and out hole number five then put another bead on. You are going to continue this the length of the comb.

Once you come out of the next to last hole, you can put your last bead on, take your cording through the last hole and then come out the next to last hole. You will notice that you have empty spaces in your comb and this is where you will fill those space.

Now you can add another bead. After you have added this bead you will need your cording to go in the next hole, if there is a bead there just gently push it out of the way, thread your cording in that hole and back out the next one. You want to make sure that while you are doing this that you are not getting your cord twisted up in your beads.

You are going to continue doing this all the way down your comb making sure that your beads stay in line. Now you can continue going back and forth down the comb using this holes adding as many beads as you want getting the cluster effect or you can simply keep it in a straight line however you do this is up to you.

Once you come to the end of the line you will have to decide whether or not go to go back down the comb with another row of beads or not. Once you have added all of the beads that you want you will need to cut off the long end of your cording until you have about 1-2 inches, whatever is easiest for you to work with. Now you will take that end and the original end that you had when you tied the cord to the comb and tie those together.

At this point it is important to note that you have to end on the same side of the comb that you began on so if you need to add another row of beads before cutting the illusion cord you should do so.

When you tie the ends together you will want to tie it twice, right over left and then left over right always works great. After you have made your knot you are going to want to grab your glue and place just a small dab on the knot. Once the glue dries you can trim down your ends that you tied together.

If you decide that you want to add more to your comb even after you have glued it you can add another piece of cording and add whatever you want to the comb. These usually look the best when they are full but it is totally up to you and your taste.

These combs are great wedding hair jewelry, look great on kids and even on adults because the vintage look is starting to come back into style. A beaded comb can take a bad hair day and turn it into a work of art so enjoy making these two projects and when you have mastered them you can move on to the next project.

Next we will earn how to bead a headband. This is a great starter project and although these beginning projects are not what most people would think of as jewelry, they are actually jewelry for your hair. Later on in the book we will get to rings, necklace and more.

Many people will tell you that you should purchase a bunch of cheap headbands, use elastic cording and just decorate them with seed beads so let's look at this option first. Cheap headbands are going to break easily as well as slip off of your head very easily. If you spend your time working on a beautiful headband you do not want it to break and you never want to have to be putting your headband back on your head.

If you are giving this as gifts you want the person you are giving them to, to enjoy them not be annoyed by them or upset because the headband was super cheap and broke within a few uses. So suggest that you spend a little extra money and purchase some good quality headbands if you are going to make these.

The next thing is using elastic cording. Many people think this is a good option because you can stretch it and make sure it is very tight but you will find that after a few used the elastic cording is going to stretch even more, your beads will become loose and the headband will look terrible. Instead make sure you purchase a good quality beading wire.

Many people choose to use the elastic cording because it is clear and does not take away from your headband. If you want to uses something that is clear but does not stretch use a heavy fishing line to bead with. You do not want to get 2 or 4 pound fishing line because it will break very easily. You also do not have to purchase the most expensive fishing line as long as it is a heavy weight.

And finally seed beads. Seed beads are great to add in between larger beads but when you are making a headband, using only seed beads can make the headband slip off of your head very easily.

When you are working with elastic headbands you want to consider how hard they are. For example, there are some elastic headbands that are very hard, for these you will be wrapping the beads onto the headband but there are also those that are very soft, you will be able to sew your beads onto those headbands.

So you will choose what type of head band you want to purchase depending on how you want to attach your beads. Of course you have the option of purchasing hard plastic headbands and wrapping beads on them as well.

When you are decorating a thin headband that you have to wrap beads onto you cannot use seed beads because they will flip around to the other side of the headband and get caught in your hair. When you wrap the beads on these headbands you want to choose a bead that is going to be the same width of the headband. You want to make sure all of the beads are the same size, flat pearls work great for this.

This is the type of headband I am talking about. As you can see it is very thin. You will need 12 inches of beads to cover the area of the headband that you will be able to see once it is on your head.

You want to try to match the color of your beads to the color of your headbands. These specific headbands come in many different colors so you don't have to worry about using only black headbands.

This first headband will take about one hour for you to make. You want to line up all of your beads before you begin stringing them.

You will need 7.5 feet of whatever cording you chose to use. Monofilament works great on this because it does not take away from the stretch of the headband. You will so need one scunci no slip grip headband such as the one pictured above. As for your beads, 7 mm o 8 mm beads seem to work the best. So basically you want to make sure that your bead from hole to hole is the same width of your headband and you will need enough of them to bead a 12 inch strip onto your headband.

That is all you will need to make the headband. Now cut out monofilament to 7.5 feet. Then you will notice that it will curl which will make it difficult for you to work with. All you have do to fix this is to take the monofilament in one hand and with the other hand pinch it, pull the monofilament through you pinched fingers several times. This will straighten it and make it much easier to work with.

Some people think that it is easier to work with shorter pieces of monofilament but personally I do not like tying off and then tying on over and over. If you prefer to work like that it is completely up to you.

The first thing you have to do is tie the monofilament onto the headband. You will notice that the headband has a seam on it, you want to put this seam underneath your beads so measure six inches to one side of the seam and that is where you will start beading. Understand that it does not have to be in the exact center of your beads but it just makes it easier for me.

To tie on you are going to pick up you first bead and thread it, place it on your headband wrapping your monofilament around the headband and threading it through the bead a second time. At this point you will need to get a ruler and make sure you are leaving a six inch tail so you can use it to tie more knots later.

Once you have measured the tail you are going to tie three knots to make sure the monofilament is secure. While you are wrapping your beads on you need to make sure you are only wrapping around one side of the head band.

Now you will work the working end of the monofilament and wrap it back under the side of the headband you are working on, then you should add the next bead. After you add each bead, you should wrap the monofilament under the band and then run it through the bead again after you run the monofilament through the bead again you will wrap it under the headband again.

Continue doing this until you have added all of your beads. On the last bead you will run through the monofilament a third time then run it under the strands of monofilament coming out of the beads. Make a loop, and run your monofilament through the loop twice then pull the knot down. Follow the thread path to the previous bead with the monofilament and before you thread through that bead, slide the monofilament under the threads going into the bead and create another knot. You will continue doing this until you only have a small piece of monofilament left. Cut the monofilament and your headband is done.

This is a very simple project but it does take some time to complete. The reason you are going to tie so many knots is so that if one comes apart you will not lose every bead on the headband, it will make it easier to fix.

Next we will talk about sewing seed beads onto a thicker softer head band.

This is the type of headband you will need to complete this project. As you can see it is much wider than the headband you just worked on.

You will also need two pieces of eight pound fire line that are each eight feet long. So you will need a total of 16 feet but since that is way too much string to work with you will cut it in half. You will also need 11 or 10 ounce seed beads. Finally you will need one size 10 beading needle.

On this specific headband where the two ends come together is bulky and it will be difficult for you to bead over so you want to make sure this is in the back of your headband. You also want to make sure that this seam is in the middle of the back of the headband so you are going to fold the headband in half at the seam and measure up 3.5 inches from the seam.

Thread your needle then pick up your headband. Insert your needle on the inside of the headband exactly where you measured the 3.5 inches from the seam to be. You want to make sure you leave about six inches of tail on this headband as well.

When you insert your needle from the back you then need to go back down with your needle you are simply creating a stich so that you can tie your thread in place. When you insert the needle to begin with, you need to make sure that you are inserting it fairly close to the edge. If you want to have seed beads all the way across your headband this is very important.

Now that you have two threads coming out the back of your headband you want to tie three knots just to ensure that it is secure. You do not want to tie the first knot really tight because it will pull on the elastic of the headband and it can actually cause a hole in the headband.

Now you are going to decide if you are going to create a pattern on your head band. If simply use some seed beads and lay the pattern out, keep the laid out pattern as a reference as you sew on seed beads. If you are not going to create a pattern you can start sewing seed beads on.

As you are sewing your beads on if you try to puncture the headband with your needle and notice it does not go through very easily you need to back the needle out because you are trying to go through the elastic. You will find that when you first start this it can take a few tries for you to figure out where you can push your needle through and where you cannot but do not go through the elastic because it will weaken the head band.

Now you will begin using your needle to pick up the amount of seed beads it will take to create a row across the headband. If you did not figure out how many beads it would take to create a row when you made your pattern you need to do that now. If you are not making any specific pattern you should pick up six seed beads with your needle, depending on the width of your headband you may have to add a few or even take a way a few.

Next you are going to insert the needle in the headband and then bring it back through the top, making sure that you are not sewing through the elastic in the headband. You will continue doing this until you have sewn all of your beads onto your headband.

Depending on how wide your headband is, this can take up to three hours but it is definitely worth it in the end. Once you finish adding your seed beads you are going to tie off. Make sure you tie off on the inside of the head band and make sure you tie a minimum of three knots. You can also make a knot after each row of seed beads you add if you want some extra security in your head band.

Beaders often do this so that if one row was to break you would only lose a few beads and you would only have to fix that specific row. Others will tell you it is not important but I like to make three knots every time I add another row of seed beads. It helps ensure the quality of our product which is very important if you are going to be selling them.

Finally to finish this chapter we are going to discuss how you can bead a hard plastic head band.

You will need the headband in the color of your choice as well as some nylon crocheting thread that is as close to the color of your headband as possible and your beads. You want to make sure that your beads are the same width as your headband or a close as possible from one hole to the other hole. You will also need a beading needle.

At this point you have two options, the first is to simply tie on your crocheting thread and start using the wrap method to place the beads on your headband but since this is a slick surface and want the best headband possible I get a bit more involved.

To make a more elegant headband you will also need a glue gun. Take the glue gun and on the inside of the headband about 1 inch from the bottom you should place a drop of glue attach the crocheting thread with this drop of glue and then begin wrapping the thread around the headband covering the area where you placed the glue.

You are then going to continue wrapping the headband until you reach the other side leaving about 1 inch just as you did on the other side. Place a small dab of glue at the end as you wrap over it. Now you can either cut the thread and start beading with fishing line or you can leave the thread and use it to bead back the other direction.

Once you have chosen what you want to do you will need to lay out your pattern of beads. You will need about 1 foot of beads depending on the size of the head band you are using. Now you will begin threading on your beads one at a time. So place your first bead on and pull it down to the headband wrap your fishing line or crocheting thread under the headband and thread the next bead. You will continue doing this until you reach the opposite end where you first started wrapping the headband. Once there you can tie off and the project is completed.

There are many variations to this project as well as all of them in this book and you can make each project your very own by adding a bit of your personality to it or changing things up all together. This is not a book of set rules so feel free to change anything in any of the directions in here.

Chapter 2
Learning how to make amazing earrings!

In this chapter I am going to take you from learning how to create easy earrings to creating amazing pieces that anyone would be proud to wear.

For these projects you are going to need a pair of round nose pliers, a nipper tool and a pair of chain nose pliers. You will also need a variety of beads, and some French wires.

Drop Earrings

The first earring we are going to make is a basic drop earring. You will need a head pin for this earring, a 24 gauge head pin is great for beginners, and they are a little softer and easier to work with. So the first thing you are going to do is simply add some beads to the head pin, and of course it will be beads that you want to make your earring out of. Then you will take your round nose pliers, place them at the top of the last bead you strung, bend the wire over the pliers at a right angle. Then wrap the wire over the top of the pliers forming a loop. Remove your round nose pliers placing them at the top of the loop, and wrap the wire around below the loop with your fingers. In some cases you may need to use your chain nose pliers. You will have a small piece of wire left that you will not be able to wrap so just clip that with your nipper tool. Then you will use your pliers to make sure the tail is tucked in.

Now you have formed your drop and the next thing you will do is to take your French wire hook, and open the loop gently with your round nose pliers by just bending it to the side, slip the drop that you created on, and close the loop. Now you have a drop earring!

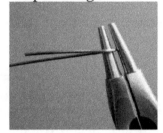

All you have to do to create the matching earring is follow the same directions I have just given you for the other, or you can make them both at the same time!

The next thing we are going to do is use an eye pin to make a pair of earrings which would be good if you want to put charms or other dangles on your earrings.

The first thing you are going to do is open the loop by gently pulling it to the side with your pliers. Place the charm in the loop and close it with your pliers. Now you are going to string whatever beads that you would like on it. After you have added your beads you are going to take your round nose pliers at the top of the last bead you added, bend the wire to a right angle, and bring the wire over, creating a loop. Grasp the loop with your pliers, and wrap the wire around below the loop just like you did in the last project.

Then you will need to trim the tail with your nipper tool. Then you can add what you have created onto your French wire by opening the loop on the French wire with your pliers, placing your drop into the loop and closing it with your pliers. Now you have created a dangle earring with a charm!

Now we are going to learn how to make an interchangeable earring. We are going to use a basic hoop earring but make different drops where you can wear multiple drops on one hoop or just one, and this will be interchangeable so you can change them as you change outfits.

The first thing we are going to do is take a head pin and add on any variety of beads that you would like to use. Sometimes you will find that your beads will have a hole that is too big and the head pin will slip through it, so often times it is best if you use a small spacer bead at the bottom of your head pin.

After you have added all of the beads, you are going to make the loop a little larger than you have on previous drops so that it wi go over the hoop earring. The way you will do this is to simply place the head pin up a bit higher on the plyer when you are bending your head pin.

Now you will create the loop just like you did in the previous tw projects. After you have created you loop all you have to do is slip it down on your hoop. You can create as many dangles as you would like and you will have an interchangeable earring.

For this next project we are going to make a chandelier earring. This is again a very simple project. There is a large variety of chandelier findings that you can pick up at your local craft stor or online, we are going to use these to create this earring.

For this project you should look for one that has three loops so you will create three drops for this earring. Just like you did with the other drop earrings you will create your three drops, and then attach them to the chandelier. After you do this you will have a chandelier earring.

Now that you have learned how to create several different styles of drop earrings we are going to move on to easy beaded stud earrings!

Beaded Stud Earrings
For this project you are going to need one large bead, 2 11/0 glass seed bead in whatever colors you choose, nylon beading thread size 00, pad studs earring posts and backs, a pair of scissors and glue.

The first thing you should do is begin with your large bead, 1/8 inch works great for this project. You want to pass the beading thread through the hole in the bead and then secure it with two knots. Remember right over left than left over right always works the best. Clip the short tail that is left after tying the beading thread around the bead with your scissors. Pass the beading thread through the hole in the large bead one more time.

Next you will begin putting your seed beads on your beading thread. Some people find it easier to do this if they thread a sewing needle with the beading thread then they can just pick up the seed beads with the tip of the needle. For a 1/8 inch bead you will need to thread 6 11/0 seed beads.

After you have the beads threaded you want to push them all the way down your thread next to your large bead then going in the opposite hole that your thread is coming out of pass the tread through the large bead again.

The next thing you will do is thread 6 more seed beads on your beading thread. You will repeat this step five times. For the second color you should pick up 5 beads at a time instead of 6 so that you will have a nice finish and the beads will not get crowded at the end.

You will want to place the sets of beads of the second color in between the rows of the first color creating a pattern. You will do this a total of 5 times so that you have no two rows of the same color together. Of course you can do this with just one color sampling stringing up 10 sets, 5 of 6 and 5 of 5. If you have enough room on your bead you can add another row or two of seed beads if you would like to.

Once you finish adding all the rows of seed beads, you will tie off your beading thread just like you would if you were sewing, making sure you tie two knots. Then you will run your thread through your bead again, pick up one bead, and run your beading tread back through the hole of the large bead. This will center one small bead over the hole of the large bead to cover the hole of the large bead and it will also cover where all of the beading thread is gathered.

After you have added the last bead you will once again create two knots just as you would if you were sewing. Make sure you pull the thread to ensure the knot is secure and then cut the beading thread.

Finally you will get your pad stud earring post, add a small drop of glue making sure it covers the entire pad, then place the back of the large bead on the pad. Hold in place for a few second to ensure it is secure then place post side up on a table to dry for a few seconds.

It takes about 10 minutes to create these gorgeous earrings and you can use as many or as few colors as you would like.

Spiral Earrings
You will need, 3 inch head pins, pliers, snippers, 2 larger beads that the head pin will fit into fairly snuggly brush on super glue and your seed beads.

The first thing you are going to do is to take your snippers and snip off the flat end of your head pin. I want to note here that if you have wire or find wire that is about the same thickness as a head pin you can use that as well, just measure it out to three inches for each earring.

Dab a bit of the super glue around the tip of the head pin or end of your wire whichever one you choose to use. If you find that the bead you want to use as the end cap is way too loose, you can let the first layer of super glue dry and just add another layer to attach the bead.

Slide your bead on and quickly swirl the bead to evenly distribute the glue, now you need to let this dry. Once your glue has dried make sure your bead is securely attached to the head pin. Do not twist the bead on purpose or it will come off.

The next thing you need to do is take your pliers and spiral your head pin. Starting with your bead in your hand you are going to grab the head pin or wire with your pliers and twist it slightly. Do this all the way down the head pen creating the spiral you want. If you find that there is not enough curve in your earring and you want more just go back and add it. Make sure you don't add more spiral than you want because it doesn't look very good when you try to straighten the wire or head pin.

Make sure you get the curve of the two earrings as close as you possible can to each other so they do look like a pair and not like they come out of two different pairs. They don't have to be exact but they should be close.

Now you can start stringing your seed beads onto your earring. This will be a little more difficult than the other earrings you have done because of the loop but once you get the hang of it you should not have a problem.

You want to leave about a quarter of an inch at the end of the spiral so you can create you loop. You will notice that the earring will get harder to bead as you get closer to the end of the wire so make sure you are holding on to them while you are adding more beads or they could start sliding off on you.

Before you create your loop just push down on the beads a little to make sure there are no gaps between them. Now grab your pliers and bend the end of our wire or head pin straight up. Make sure you hold the earring so that you are looking down on it as if it is being worn and bend the head pin or wire up and not out. You want to make a 90 degree angle when bending your wire.

Now you need to create a loop just like you did with the drop earrings you already made so that you can attach the beaded wire to the actual earring. Open up the loop on the earring and hang your spiral on it. Close the loop and you are done!

Super Easy Beautiful Earring
As you can see by the heading this is going to be a super easy very beautiful earring that you can make. First you will need five head pins for each earring, one 6mm loop per earring 2 different types of beads, 5 of each for each earring. By this I mean for example one large black bead and one smaller pearl bead, you will need a total of 10 of each to complete the pair of earrings. You will need your pliers and the actual earring that will go through your ear. This project is going to leave a

lot of the creativity up to you but you will definitely enjoy doing it and you will enjoy the final product. You will need wire cutters as well.

To start off you are going to leave one of your headpins the length it is, take two head pins and cut them slightly shorter than the first head pin, then take the last two and cut them about half the length of the first head pin.

The next thing you are going to do is thread your beads onto each pen in whatever pattern you like but making sure the pattern stays the same on all of the beads.

Create a loop at the end of your head pens after you have placed your beads. Place all of the loops into the 6mm loop in this pattern, small medium, large, medium and finally small. Open the loop on the earring and place the 6mm loop inside, close the earring loop and you are done!

You can make a ton of different cascading earrings by using this patter and since it is so easy it really is one of my favorite ways to make gorgeous earrings.

Swirling Earrings
This next project will create a beautiful earring as well, and is easy enough for even beginners. At this point I would think of you not as a beginner at earring making but even if you are still learning and struggling just a little you will be able to make this project with no problem.

To begin you will need some size 11 seed beads. Three feet of fire line for the entire earring, three larger beads, and a size 10 or 12 needle.

Now you want to pick up four seed beads with your needle, you will already have you stopper bead connected to your thread at this point so you want to bring your seed beads down the fire line until you are about 1 inch above the stopper bead. Insert your needle in through those beads again from the bottom to the top. You will a third time insert your needle into the beads at the bottom but only catch two beads this time. Now you will notice all of the beads have been brought together. Your bottom thread will be coming out of only one bead at this point. Find the bead that is directly opposite of the bead your bottom thread is coming out of and run your needle though it so the threads come out on opposite sides.

Now instead of picking up four beads with your needle you are going to pick up three using the bead that your thread is coming out of as the fourth. With your beads on the needle and not pushed down the tread you need to take your needle and insert it into the opposite side of the bead that your thread is currently coming out of. If you insert the needle into the side of the bead that the thread is coming out of you will simply unravel your beads so make sure you pay attention.

Now you want to pass your needle through the next two beads in the group brining all together and allowing you to build on it once again. Pick up three more beads with your needle and continue the same pattern until you have 16 sets on your thread.

The way you will count how many sets of beads you have is that each set will have beads that stick out from the thread on each side. Choose one side and count those beads that stick out they will represent one set.

Once you have all 16 sets made you will go through one more bead so that your thread is coming out of one of the beads along the edge that sticks out.

Now you will need some size 8 seed beads pick up one with your needle, and simply pass your needle through the next seed bead that is sticking out on the side. That is all you are going to do all the way down the project. Since you are placing a larger seed bead in this empty space you will be creating a curve. Once you have added the size 8 beads all the way down you will sew through the end bead and turn your work around, this will put you on the other side of the project.

Go through the first seed bead that is sticking out on this side and now you will need size 15 seed beads. Do the same thing with these as you did the size 8 seed beads. This is going to build on your curve because now you are working with a smaller seed bead.

You will do this all the way to the end of this side. Make sure you are only go through one bead at a time and make sure your thread does not loop around any other beads as you are beading.

Now that you have completed this part you can remove your stopper bead you added when you began but make sure you don't cut the tail all the way off.

Push your needle through the seed bead that is right on the tip of the project again. Then you will push your needle through the center hole that has been created from the first four size 11 beads. Now you will need 3 pearls. Pick up one 15, one pearl and one 15, then you will count the center of the sets, were the center hole is not counting the one your thread is coming out of, count five more.

Push your needle through the center of that set and pull it all together. Pick up a 15, a pearl and a 15 on your needle, and do the same thing, not counting the set you are coming out of count five and push your needle through the center of the set, pulling it all together. Pick up a 15, pearl and a 15. Go through the center of the very last set with your needle.

This is your earring base. Now you want to reinforce the earring because there is only one thread holding the center together at this point so push your needle through the tip seed bead once again, then push your needle through the center hole on the top set of your earring and simply pass it through all of the beads in the center of the earring. It is much easier said than done and it could take you a few minutes to do this. Don't worry because even the most seasoned beaders often have trouble with this. You may have to take it one bead at a time and that is perfectly okay. Once you get to the other end, go back through the center section.

Anchor the little tip seed bead by going through it once more. Pick up six of your 15 seed beads with your needle and slide a 4mm closed jump ring onto your needle as well. Then push your needle back through that tip seed bead once more to create a loop. Now you need to reinforce this at least twice more so simply sew through those seed beads a few more times. Now just find an area where you can make a knot in between your beads and create a knot, make sure this does not go over a bead. Move up two beads and do it again. Do this three or four times.

After you have created your knots pass your needle through two or three beads then cut your thread. Open up your earring hook with your pliers, place the 4mm loop in the opened earring hook and close. Now you have completed one earring. Follow the same directions for the opposite earring.

Chain Earring

Now I am going to show you how to make a chain earring with a dangle. You are going to need some premade chain. You can use whatever thickness you like so if you like a heavier chain go ahead and use that, and if you like a lighter chain that will work with this as well.

You will need five inches of chain per earring to start out with. Next you will cut about 2 inches of wire and thread it through your bead so your bead is about 1/3 of the way down the wire, using your fingers you will bend the wire into a U shape. Then take one tail of the U and cross it over the other tail so you have an open loop. Take that same end of the tail and wrap it the rest of the way around the other tail creating a loop. You will then have one straight wire sticking up and will be able to see the dangle you just created at the end.

About half way down this straight wire you are going to take your round needle nose pliers and create a coil slide this into the bottom link of your 5 inch chain. Once this is done all that you have to do is create as many of these dangles as you want, and attach them along the sides of your chain. When you have about five of them total or however many you want, you will decide how long you want the earring to be.

The great thing about this earring is that you can make it really long it dangles just above your shoulders, you can make it medium length or you can make it short it is all about what you like. Choose how long you are going to make the earring, cut the next link in the chain and separate the two pieces. Open up the loop on the earring hook and slide the chain link through the loop. Close and you are finished! How easy was that?

 The great thing about making beaded earrings is that they can be so simple, of course there are more difficult ones and depending on how much time you want to take you can make these as well.

Creating earrings is a simple project that almost anyone can do, you can be as creative as you want and it does not take a lot of time to make something beautiful. Your friends and family will love getting your creations on birthdays or during special occasions.

Once you have learned how to make basic earrings, there are tons of things you can do to jazz up your earrings just a little bit. Start with using bead caps, they are exactly what they sound like, small caps that you put on the top and bottom of your beads to make them a bit prettier.

Bead caps come in tons of colors, metals and designs so you can always find something to add to your designs.

Double it up. After you have created one dangle, use an eye pin and create more attach these to your earring by opening the loop of the earring and sliding the eye pin on. You can use eye pens of different lengths to add character to your earrings. Make each of the dangles a little different for a new style.

Use a larger jump ring if your earring loop is to add the number of dangles you want. You can also try different earring hooks when you are making your earrings. Don't just stick with one, try out a few and see what a difference it makes.

When cutting your wire one end will be sharp and the other will be flat, always make sure that you use the flat end to create your loop that will connect your dangle to your ear hook.

Also make sure that you close your loops all the way, often beginners will leave their loops just slightly open and will end up losing all of their wonderful creations.

Make sure when you are grasping your wire with your pliers that you are not grasping to tightly or you will mark you wire, this will be visible in your earring.

Finally, make sure you are taking your time when it comes to making earrings. You are not going to become a pro overnight and you will make mistakes. This is perfectly normal and it is okay don't let it frustrate you slow down and try again.

If you find you are struggling, take a step back and walk away from the project until you have cleared your mind and can focus on the project at hand. Creating beaded earrings is a great way to relax but if you take it too seriously it can cause a ton of stress in your life. You don't want your hobbies to cause stress and if you are creating earrings that you want to sell, your customers will be able to tell which earrings you enjoyed creating and which ones stressed you out.

Chapter 3

How to make lovely necklaces.

The first necklace we are going to learn how to make is a multi-strand necklace for beginners. After we finish this we will work our way up to some more complex necklaces but we will make sure to work in some simple projects along the way.

Some basic supplies that you will need are: a bead board, which is a plastic tray that has measurements on it and comes in very handy. If you do not have a bead board a towel on your table will work just fine. You will also need some bead stringing wire in what ever color you choose. You will also need a crimp bead, it should tell you on your wire spool which crimp bead you will need. You use a crimp bead to secure wire because you cannot knot it.

You will also need a clasp for your necklace. What I recommend for a beginner is to buy an assortment pack so you can try out a few and then decide which type is your favorite to work with before buying larger packages of one specific clasp.

Of course you will need beads of different sizes as well as different colors. You want to make sure you have a lot of smaller beads so that you can use them as filler bids.

Now that you have all of your supplies together you will want to cut off about 50 inches of wire since this is going to be a multi-strand necklace. Then you are going to take one end of your clasp, and put the wire through putting the clasp in about the middle of your wire. You will want your strands staggered so yo will want one end to be just a little bit shorter. You should note that you will be cutting off some excess wire at the end and you can save those scraps for making earrings or bracelets depending on how much is left over.

To secure your clasp you will want to put on a crimp bead. Simply thread both ends of the wire through the crimp bead an slide it up pretty close to the clasp. Then you want to separate the wires making sure they are not crossed, and use your pliers to crimp the bead. Now there is a tool made for crimping and it costs around 20 dollars but you do not have to have the tool. If you are trying to make very professional looking necklaces and you will be making a lot of them you should consider purchasir the crimping tool.

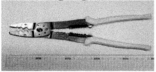

Now that you have your clasp attached you want to lay out you design. You can use a mixture of beads to make the necklace exactly how you want it to look. You want to put a few small beads on first because it will make it easier to clasp the necklace once it is finished.

You can lay out the design before you make the necklace or you can create a random design as you go. If you start off random, make sure you finish random and making a random design lets your artistic abilities flow and is very fun.

The first beads that you are putting on should be something like seed beads. Now these will be covered by your hair but it is much more comfortable to have these beads on the necklace than to make a necklace without them because the wire will rub on your neck.

After you have strung about 10 seed beads you can begin your design, place your first larger bead on your necklace followed by about 4 seed beads. String your next few beads, followed by more seed beads. This part of the necklace is completely up to you, you want to continue stringing beads until you have the length that you want. You want to finish up by adding the same amount of seed beads you started off with so for this project the last 10 beads should be seed beads.

Now you need to slide on a crimp bead to the strand you just finished, string your clasp, and push your wire through the crimp bead again. Some people like to use two crimp beads just in case one breaks they know that they have the extra security of the second crimp bead. This is a very good idea if you are making necklaces to sell because it will ensure that you are not selling products that will fall apart. Make sure before you crimp your crimp bead that your wires are not crossed.

After you have crimped your crimp bead you can cut the wire and begin threading the second strand of your necklace. You want to keep the second strand very simple and plain so that the eye will focus on the first strand. Once you get to the end of this strand you will put the crimp bead on the exact same way you did on the first strand and you will have a completed multi-strand necklace.

Floating wire necklace

For our next necklace project we are going to work on a floating wire necklace. If you want to use a light colored wire with this project that is fine but if you have a nice colored wire that you really want to show off, this is a great way to do so. We are also going to attach some chain to the end of this necklace just to create a nice quick finished ending.

You will need .012 beading wire, or .015 if you want the wire to be a little bit thicker, you will also need two crimp beads or tubes which ever you prefer. You will also need some chain. This necklace will be about 24 inches when you are finished with it so it will sit nicely above a sweater and you will be able to just slip it over your head without needing a clasp.

To start this necklace you need to cut four pieces of your wire, you can go ahead and attach one end to your chain at this point if you know exactly how long you want your necklace to be or you can just use a bead stopper until you have finished with your necklace design.

Now you want to separate all of you wires so you can see the individually, the wire that is furthest to the right will be wire 1, going to the left of wire 1 you will have wires 2, 3, and 4. This is simply so you will know which wire I am talking about.

The first thing you are going to do is put a bead on wire 1 and let it drop down next to your bead stopper, then pick up wires 1 and 2 adding a bead to those wires allowing that bead to drop down next to the first bead. Now you are going to pick up wires 2 and 3. Place your bead on wires 2 and 3 then pick up wires 3 and 4. Add your bead to the 3 and 4 wires pushing it up to the beads you have already added. Then you are going to add a bead to wire 4 by itself.

So at this point you have put a bead on wire 1 by itself, 1 and 2 together, 2 and 3 together, 3 and 4 together than just 4 by itself. All you are going to do now is just continue to repeat that pattern so you are going to put a bead on wire 1, a bead on wires 1 and 2, a bead on wires 2 and 3, a bead on wires 3 and 4, and finally a bead on wire for by itself.

All you are going to do is continue with this pattern all the way down the necklace and it will create a nice little netting effect. You will end the beading with one bead on wire 1 and one bead on wires 1 and 2. Now you are ready to add your chain. You should know that the beads will float around on this necklace so do not be alarmed if they move around on you a bit while you are adding your chain.

Now you want to cut about 10 inches of chain depending on how long you want your necklace, grab all of your wires together, and put on your crimp tube or bead. For this project a 2x2 crimp tube will work the best because it will fit all four strands into it. Next you need to take all four strands of wire through your last chain link, then push all four wires back through the crimp tube Pull the tube and wires to make sure they are all secure, make sure there is not at ton of excess wire on your necklace and crimp the tube. Now you can cut off the excess wire. To make up for any extra wire on your necklace just push all of the beads down on the wire making more wire on the other side.

Before you do anything else you want to make sure you don't have any gaps in your necklace, if you do just push your beads down where they belong. Now you will gather all four of your wires and if they are not even you need to trim them all even. Now you can add your crimp tube and the other side of your chain. When you add your crimp tube to this side you want to drop it down close to your beads.

After you have added your chain and cut off the excess wire you have finished your floating wire necklace. You can also add a clasp if that is something that you like or make the chain shorter or longer. You can also make the beaded part of the necklace as long as you would like. You may decide that you want to add more wires and if this is the case, just make sure you continue following the beading pattern through all of your wires ensuring that the first and the last wire always get a bead of their own.

We are going to make one more necklace project in this chapter before moving on to the next chapter where we will talk about making bracelets and end the book learning how to make our very own rings. The next project we will work on is a Russian spiral necklace. You can also make a very cute matching bracelet following the same directions on a smaller scale.

Russian Spiral Necklace

For this project I am going to teach you how to create the Russian spiral, I think we have gone over adding clasps and chains enough that I will not have to discuss that for this necklace but I do want to spend some time discussing the Russian spiral because it make a beautiful necklace or bracelet.

The minimum materials you will need for this project is a size 15 o's seed bead and a size 8/o's seed bead. For this project I will be teaching you how to use three different colors of 8/o's and one color of 15/o's. You will also need .006 beading thread. When you choose the colors of the beads you will be using than you will match your thread to the color scheme of your beads. You will also need a size 12 beading needle.

To start out you will need to dump out and make piles of your seed beads so you will be able to string them quickly. You will want to cut your thread, you will start out with about five feet of thread cut but you will be using more than this because it is a very thread intensive necklace. Now you are going to use your beading needle to begin picking up your beads. You will start out with the 8/o's. Using your needle you should pick up your first color of seed bead and follow it by two of the 15/O seed beads, pick up the second color followed by two 15/o seed beads, pick up the third color and follow it buy two of the 15/O seed beads.

After you thread this on your needle you are going to let them drop down close to the end of your thread. Now pick up the beads that you just let slide close to the end of your thread and you want to tie them in a round, you will want to do this if you are adding a clasp if on the other hand you are not and just wa this to be a slip over necklace or bracelet, you will loop the thread so the beads actually become the loop and sew through your first set of 8/O and 2 15/O's then pull tight.

Now you will need your needle to come out between two 15/O beads so you need to sew through the beads until you reach this point. Once you have your thread coming out of this point you are going to start creating another set of beads. Whatever color is closest to the seed bead your thread is coming out of is the color you will start this set with in order to get the spiral of the Russian spiral.

So you will add your colored 8 seed bead, two 15's then you have to sew again, you will skip over the seed bead that is next to the one your thread is coming out of, skip over the 8, and sew into the next 15. This will make sure that again your needle is coming out between 2 15's. Now you will add your next bead. It will be the same color as the 8 bead that you just skipped over, followed by two 15's. Now you will do the exact same thing you did for the last set, skip over the next 15 and the 8 sewing through the next 15. At this point it will look a little messy but once you get really going you will see it turn into a work of art. The next bead you should put on will be the color of the 8 that you just skipped over followed by 2 15's, and sew through the first 15 that you were coming out of in the beginning. At this point you will have an odd shape of beads but as you add more it will become more rounded.

At this point you will need to do a step up which is what will take you to the next row. Right now you should be coming out of the original 15 that you started with you want to push your needle through your first 8/O and your first 15/O of your second go around making sure you come out between two 15's.

That is how you are going to step up so each time when you are finished putting on your three rotations of your beads you are going to do that step up. You are going to continue to follow this pattern.

Once you finish the third row you will begin to see the color spiral just a little bit. After you get a couple rows completed this becomes very easy and almost a mindless project but in the beginning it can be very difficult. This project is also very time consuming but the end product is worth it.

So you will continue this sewing pattern making sure you do a step up with each completed rotation. Once you get to the end of this piece of thread you will have to decide if you want to continue on or finish if you continue on just tie your two pieces of yarn together, and if you want to finish this is where you would add your chain or clasp. If you are creating a pull over necklace, you will want to sew the two ends of your necklace together making sure that you pull the knots tight so they do not come loose.

Of course there are literally hundreds if not thousands of different types of necklaces you can create and these are just a few examples. You can make something as simple as a charm corded necklace to something as complex as the Russian spiral necklace. Whatever you decide to make it will be something that you can be proud of and something that you can enjoy spending time doing. '

To finish this chapter I want to give you a few more beading tips. The first thing I want to talk about is keeping your knots tight and your jewelry looking nice. If you have loose beads or loose knots your jewelry is going to look like it was made by a child. Take the time to make sure you are tying strong tight knots and that you are keeping your beads close together with no unwanted gaps.

Many times people will go out and purchase beading kits, I don't recommend this. It is my opinion that you should take the time to pick out all of your beads on your own. Now this does not go for seed beads. You want to grab a lot of different seed beads for your projects and these kits often come with a great container to store your seed beads. The only problem is that these are often cheaper seed beads and you need to watch that you do not use two that are stuck together as well as watch the size of the beads. When you buy kits like this, you will end up getting several sizes of beads that say they are one specific size.

When you first unroll your thread, wire or fire line it will tend to curl on you can straighten it by running it through your thumb and your index finger a few times.

Sometimes you will grab the wrong bead with your needle often times people think they can just go back through the beads the attached to get the bead off. This will not work, it will only create a bigger mess. Instead take the needle off of your thread and give the beads a tug, they will slide right off or your thread or and you can simply rethread your needle and put the correct beads on.

If you try to go back through the beads with your needle you will create a knot, at this point you will have to cut your thread and start the beading over.

Before you take on a large or difficult project when it comes to necklaces, you want to make something fairly simple start with a few rows of seed beads possibly throwing in a few larger beads as you go. Get the feel for beading before you try something difficult.

Don't try to bead without the proper equipment. Don't try to bead with no wire cutters, pliers and other supplies. Don't skimp on your supplies either. Often I see beaders who really want to create something great but they won't spend money to get great beads. If cost is a problem when you are first starting out search the internet for some great deals. You can usually get your beads at about 90 percent off what you would pay at a craft store.

Buy a pack of earring hooks or necklace clasps that contains several different types this way you can try out several kinds and find which one you like the best.

Let your creativity flow. Once you learn the basics of how to make earrings, let your creativity flow and start creating your own. You don't have to make earrings that have already been made by someone else. Start by mixing up colors, adding to the length or just creating an entirely new design.

If you are making a necklace with a chain and you want to make something a little different, add a ribbon to the back of it. You can use this to clasp the necklace as well.

Chokers are coming back into style, add a few dangling beads to a ribbon or piece of lace and you have a beautiful choker.

While you are making your bracelets don't for get to make some matching anklets.

Speaking of matching why not create a pair of earrings, a necklace, a bracelet and ring to all wear together. If you are selling your jewelry you will find that people love sets like this.

Don't spend a ton of money on patterns for your jewelry now that you know the basics just search for what you want to make online, people are posting new jewelry making videos every day

Don't let jewelry making take over your life. I have seen it so often, someone picks up a new hobby, they spend all of their time working on the hobby and let everything else fall to the side. Even if you think you are going to make money you still have a life to live, make sure you are socializing, exercising and actually having a life outside of jewelry making. If you would like you can start a jewelry making group in order to make new friends who also enjoy your new hobby.

Ask for help when you don't understand something. One of the greatest things about the internet is that we can reach out and ask for help from those who have a lot more experience than we do. There are tons of online groups you can join and lots of people willing to share their experiences as well as their knowledge with you.

Finally if you want to start selling your jewelry start small, work a few craft shows or set up a booth at the farmers market, see if you are making what people are looking for. You can also post a few items online for sell and see if anyone bites. If it takes off you can grow your business but if it does not you really haven't lost anything.

Chapter 4
Learning how to make bracelets

Making bracelets is a great way to learn how to make very complex pieces that are beautiful but small. Many of these projects can be turned into necklaces if you continue on with the beading.

The bracelet we are going to make is a very beautiful bangle that is embellished. If at any time you feel like this project is just too much for you at this time take a step back and go work through some of the older projects again until you feel comfortable moving on to the harder ones. This project is quite complex so it will be the only project in this chapter.

This is going to be a cubic red angle weave bangle bracelet so if you hear anyone talk about cubic red angle weave this is what they are talking about.

In order to make this project you are going to need two colors of 4mm round beads, about 135 of each color, 11/0 seed beads, and about 111 4mm bicone crystals of course the amount of beads you will need with very depending on the size of your bracelet.

To get started you will need to thread a couple of yards of fire line onto your beading needle. Then pick up four of one color of your beads with your needle. Make sure you leave about a 12 inch tail once you have your beads on the thread. At this point you are going to sew back up through all of the beads that you have added. Pull your thread so you have a small loop, ½ made of beads, ½ made of only thread. Then you want sew through the very first bead that you added one more time.

After you sew through this bead you will pull the thread tight. Now you will have a small set of four beads which will be your base. You want to go ahead and sew through this again so that your base does not fall apart. Finish sewing through in the bead that is opposite of the tail you left.

Now using your needle pick up one of your second color bead, one of the first color bead, and another second color bead. Now you are going to sew through the opposite side of the bead that your thread is coming out of. Pull the thread tight and move to the next bead on your base, sew through the bead.

Now you want to pick up one bead of color 2 and one of color 1 with your needle. Now this is where it gets a little tricky. You are going to have one bead of color two on the side of your unit you have created that your thread is coming out of. I want you to go back with your needle and sew it through that bead of color two entering the right side of the bead and exiting the left side. As you exit the left side of the bead you need to enter the next base bead with your needle and exit it as well.

Pull your thread tight and all of your color 2 beads should be in a row. What you are creating here is called the wall and ceiling to your base or floor. This will make more sense as the bracelet comes together but it is important to know what they are called. The second color you are adding is actually called your wall color and if you stand the beads up as the wall of the cube you can see that the second color will create the wall of the cube and the base color will create the ceiling of the cube.

At this point your thread should be coming out of your base unit or floor again so you want to push the needle through the next base bead that is in line. Now you are going to pick up one of the color 2 beads and one of the color one beads just like you did on the last step. And just like you did in the last step sew through the color two bead and then through the base bead.

Now you will have to create what is called the fourth wall and this is where may people get confused. You want to sew through the last base bead, and the closest color 2 bead to the right, use your needle to pick up a color one bead, then sew through the color two bead that is to the left of your base bead as well as through the base. Once you have done this, if you have done it correctly, it will pull everything together. You will have what looks like a small blob of beads. But you will be able to see what is meant by walls, floors and ceilings.

Now your thread should still be coming out of the base but we need to get it to the ceiling in order to secure them so you are simply going to travel up the wall, sewing through the color 2 bead that is above your base bead, and then just sew through all of the beads on the top. This will secure your ceiling and close it in.

Once you close in the ceiling it will become your floor or base for you to add your next unit to. The way you do this is to follow the same directions as you did to create the walls and ceiling of the last unit. You will continue to follow this pattern until you have reached your desired length. The way to determine how long you want the bracelet to be is to take a piece of string and wrap it around the widest part of your hand then measure the length and add about one inch to that.

The reason you add an inch is because this bracelet will take up some space on your wrist and once you embellish it, it will lose some of its length.

Once you have made the bracelet the length that you want it to be you are going to join the two ends into a bangle. The way you do this is to thread your needle with your tail that you left when you started, you are going to join the ends with the tail and then come back through with the working end of your thread in order to create a very strong connection.

You should have ended your bracelet on the same bead you started it with so you will notice that you will have like beads on both ends. These are the floor and ceiling to this cube, all you have to do now is add the walls. So you will pick up bead color two with your needle, and sew into the exact opposite bead on the other side of the bracelet. Thread another color 2 bead, and sew into the exact opposite bead that you are coming out of, it will be the same bead your thread was coming out of before adding the previous bead. Then you will sew into the next wall bead, and the floor bead. Next you will turn your bracelet to the next side and connect it the same way there.

The only difference is that you will already have one wall done on this side so you only need to add one color two bead. After you have added this bead you will sew through the wall bead that was already there and through the floor bead. Sew through the next floor bead and add another color 2 bead. Sew through the ceiling bead, through the wall bead that was already there and then back through the floor bead.

Now you will turn to your next side, at this point all four of your beads should already be there so all you have to do is sew through them all and secure them. After you come out of the last bead you are going to pull everything tight and make a knot using the connecting thread of one of the close beads.

Sew down into the unit that your knot is next to and make another not using the tread bridge. You want to continue to do this until you run out of tail thread.

Now that you have sewn in your tail and tied it off you are going to find your working thread and add some embellishments. At this point you will see that you have created a beautiful bangle bracelet so if you want to keep it as it is that is fine but if you want to add some embellishment you will really love it when it is finished.

Now you want to sew until your working thread is coming out of one of the color two beads on the top of your bracelet so that you are ready to sew between two color 2 beads on the top side of your bracelet.

Once you have done this pick up 2 11/0 seed beads, and sew into the next color 2 bead in the line. You are going to do this all the way around filling in the spaces between the color two beads.

Once you finish sewing on all of your seed beads your thread will be coming out of the side of your bracelet now you want to sew through a side bead and through one of the color two beads. On the inside of the bracelet we are going to use one 11/0 seed bead instead of two. You will do the exact same thing you did for the top only using one seed bead instead of two all the way around.

Now that you have finished this round you want to sew through a side bead and through a color two bead making sure your thread is coming out of the color two bead. Now you are going to continue to put one seed bead in between each of the color two beads on this side. Again you will do this all the way around the bracelet.

Next you will once again sew through a side bead sewing your way back to the top but on the opposite side that you sewed the two seed beads on. Making sure you are coming out of a color two bead you will sew two seed beads in between each color two bead.

Once you have finished adding all of your seed beads you want to take your needle and sew through the color one bead that is closest and pull through. Now you are going to start your top embellishments.

With your needle pick up an 11/0 seed bead, a 4mm bicone, and another seed bead. Once you have these on your thread you are going to sew into the next bead on the opposite side of where your thread is coming out. So you will create a diagonal with the thread. Pull your thread and you will have a cute diagonal design. You will repeat this the entire length of the bracelet.

After you have finished the top you are going to do the same thing on the sides of the bracelet. You will want to make your diagonal on the side go the opposite way as the diagonal on the top. Once you finish one side you will sew through the bottom beads to get to the opposite side of the bangle so you can embellish it.

After you have done the second side, sew what is left of your thread into your bracelet making knots as you go just like you did when you were tying off the tail of the tread. Your project is complete! This is a beautiful bracelet and it is something you can be proud to say you made!

beads-beading-needs.com

A Few Tips

Simplify. Often people will put so many beads on a project that it becomes cluttered and over complicated. Instead try creating something simple and elegant. If you find that you are creating a ton of overly complex pieces, take a step back and get back to basics with some simple but pretty pieces.

Make sure your beads match. One thing that drives me crazier than anything when it comes to beading is when people do not make sure that their beads match. For example, don't use expensive crystals with plastic looking seed beads. Lay your pattern out before you start it and make sure the beads look good together.

Use old beads to make something new. When you find you have a ton of pieces filling up your jewelry box and you are not wearing them any more, go ahead and take them apart, use the beads to create something new. There is no need for those beautiful beads to be sitting in a box and not being worn by anyone.

Start out by making jewelry for yourself as well as for your friends and family. This is very important if you want to sell your projects in the future. Your friends and family will give you an honest opinion about your work and by creating projects for yourself, you will find out if you are creating a quality product that does not fall apart. It is much better to have a bracelet that you are wearing fall apart on you than one fall apart you have sold to your customer.

You can earn a great income by selling your hand beaded jewelry but don't quite your day job right away. Many people will jump right into something like this and go full force right away. I suggest that you create beaded jewelry and sell it in your spare time until you are making enough money to actually quit your job. You don't want to put yourself into debt or lose everything you own because you tried to jump into a beading business when you were not ready.

Store all of your beading supplies together and out of children's reach. Beads can be a choking hazard to little kids so you want to make sure they cannot reach them. Children can also get injured from many of the supplies that are used when beading so you need to keep all of this stuff put away as well. Another reason you want to keep it all put away is because it can become very frustrating when you want to work on a project and you can not find all of your supplies. The last reason you want to keep it put away is even if you do not have beads large enough for a child to choke on they are going to be attracted to the cool shinny beads in all the different colors you have. Kids tend to spill things and mix beads up as well. It can become quite stressful if you have 50 different color and size beads all dumped into one pile. If your seed beads get mixed up you may never get them sorted out again.

Don't give up when you face struggles. If you make a necklace and it falls apart, make sure you reinforce the next one, if you make a head band and it comes unraveled, consider using a little bit of super glue on the inside to keep it together next time. Find out what you did wrong so you don't do it again in the future.

Never stop learning. There are tons of websites that will teach you so much that you can use when it comes to making beaded jewelry. This book covers a lot, more than most books out there but of course I cannot cover everything. People are coming out with new techniques, new designs everyday and they want to share them with you. If you take just an hour per week and devote it to learning more about creating beaded jewelry you will pick up a ton of information.

Take notes, not just when you are watching a video or reading online but even while you read through this book. One of the best ways I have found that I can retain information that I will need in the future is to take notes. This is why teachers used to push it so hard when you were in school, you can listen to a video or read a book and retain some information but if you tal notes you will retain even more. Use this in all of your life not just when you are beading.

Reflect your style in your work. You may think if you are wanting to sell your pieces that others will not like your style but people are interested in not only buying but seeing interesting and creative pieces on you. Don't smother your creativity just because you think others will not like it.

When you are beading on a budget you need to understand that all beads are not created equal. If you buy cheap beads you may find that they not only crack while you are working with them which can be upsetting but they an also crack while your friends, families or buyers are wearing them. It is understandable that you want to save money while you learn how to create pieces but purchasing the super cheap beads is not the way to go. Now this is not to say you should not purchase beads when they are on sale or on clearance, one of the best places I have found to buy beads often sells them for much less than other stores because they go on clearance this is when I stock up. I have bought from this store many times and I know they sell quality beads. You may have to work with a few brands at first before you know what brand you want to continue to purchase and what brands you are just wasting money on. One way to get around this is to ask people online who bead where they get their beads and if they have had any issues. I found my beading store from a video online where a woman was just raving about how little she had to pay for her beads. Do a bit of research of course and make sure that whoever you buy from is a real company since there are so many scams online you want to make sure you are safe. And if all possible pay with PayPal, this way they cannot access your bank or credit card information and you can ask for a refund through PayPal if there is an issue.

Throw a beading party. Often times we forget to involve our friends in our new hobbies, to prevent this, invite everyone over, have them bring some beads and show them how to create all the amazing pieces you have learned.

Designate a work space that is only going to be used for your jewelry making. It does not have to be an entire room, or a desk, it can be a small table in the corner of your living room where you do your beading. It needs to be clear to the rest of the people in your house that this is not a place to hang out or do home work or mess around it, it is your area where you will be doing your beading. It needs to be left alone.

Keep your beading area clean and tidy. Think about this, you want to make a few pieces, you go to your work area and find it pile up with junk that you never got around to putting away. Are you still going to feel like being creative and making some great pieces or are you going to choose to go back to the couch because the area was a mess? When ever you finish creating pieces, make sure you put everything away all of your beads and all of your supplies. Then do not place stuff on this desk or table. It is not for mail you haven't read or bills you need to pay. Find another area in the house for things like that.

Practice, practice, practice. No matter what it is that you are trying to learn, you need to make sure you get enough practice. As the old saying goes, practice makes perfect and it is no different with beading. Practice threading your needles, practice picking up beads with your wire as well as your needle. Practice tying small knots practice creating loops with your wire. Practice bending your wire without marking it. There are so many things you can take the time to practice on that you could literally fill up all of your free time. I understand that no one wants to sit around and practice all of this stuff but if you do not practice these techniques you work will look sloppy and will fall apart.

Take pictures of your jewelry. This is important if you are going to be selling or giving it away. You may think back to a piece that you created and forget exactly how it turned out. If you take pictures you will also be able to tell over time how much you have evolved in your style as well as quality. This is also important if you tell someone they are getting a one of a kind piece. You can also use these pictures on websites later on if you want to start selling your jewelry or create small flyers to hand out advertising your jewelry locally.

Check out Pinterest for the latest designs. Pinterest is great if you are in to DIY crafting or beading and there are tons of pins that have to do with the newest available beads as well as new techniques. Many of these people who create these pins have websites that focus on making beaded jewelry so make sure you look for a few to follow.

Place your beads on a silicone baking sheet while you are creating your pieces. The silicone will hold onto the beads so they do not end up rolling around on you while you are trying to get them on your needle. Choose a contrasting color of your beads so they are easier to see. This will make beading go much faster for you.

Use your beads to add a bit of flare to your wardrobe. Simply sew the beads to the colors or cuffs of your shirts or even the pockets of your pants to jewel them up a bit and add a little of your own style.

If you buy assorted beads that come in one bag often it is great to purchase a few extra muffin pans. You can spray paint these pans so they do not get mixed in with the ones you use for cooking and sort your beads out in them. They are also great for storing beads that you don't have room for in your bead boxes.

Many people purchase bead boxes from a crafting store but did you know you can get the same container much cheaper if you purchase them in the fishing department at your local big box store? Also if you have a husband who likes to fish you can get them with rubber worms in them, these are still cheaper than at the craft stores and all you have to do is put the rubber worms in a plastic baggy for your husband or boyfriend. One note, make sure you wash your hands before you touch the worms, you don't want to get perfumes or lotions on the worms and your husband will thank you for being so careful and considerate.

Those are all of the tips I have for you for now, in the next chapter you are going to learn how you can make wonderful beaded rings but that is not all. At the end of the chapter I have added a few bonuses for you. One is how to make your very own beads out of newspaper or any type of paper for that matter, followed by how you can make bead balls and ending with how to make a bead ball necklace.

Chapter 5
How to make wonderful rings.

As I have walked through the stores I have noticed that many are selling big chunky rings. The fact is that kids are not the only ones wearing this and they are a great way to make a bold fashion statement. But instead of paying 20 dollars per ring why not make some yourself (and maybe even sell a few!!)

None of the rings in this chapter are extremely difficult so we will be going over several different projects. At the end of this chapter I will discuss a few tips for you when it comes to making handmade beaded jewelry.

The first ring we are going to make is the simple wire wrap beaded ring. To create this ring you will need a ring mandrel, snipe or chain nose pliers, snips and a ruler. You will also need a large bead about 8mm will work the best, 12 inches of .8mm or 20 gauge round silver wire.

Once you have your wire measured out you need to just make sure it is straightened out because it makes the project a little easier. You want to make a mark on the center of your wire with a marker and once you put your bead on the wire make sure you line it up with the mark.

Once you have centered your bead, bend the sides of the wire down so that the bead cannot move. Now you will place the wire and bead on the ring mandrel. Hold the bead with your thumb and wrap the wires around so they are around the mandrel and back to the front of the ring. It should look a bit like the spring, you need to make sure that the wires do not cross over.

Once you get the wire back to the front with the bead you are going to grab both pieces of wire and start wrapping both around the bead at the same time wrapping counter clockwise. Three times will be plenty for this ring but if you want to have more wire on your ring just cut it longer when you begin the project.

At this point you will notice that there is a gap between the bead and the wrap that you have created so the way you fix this is to take the ring off of the mandrel and instead of grabbing both wires at this point you are just going to grab one pulling it up close to the bead as you wrap it. And do the same thing with the other wire.

This will give you a much more professional look, instead of having a very visible wire that goes through the bead, it looks like the bead is nestled in the wire.

Now take the wire and wrap it around the shank of the ring, then depending on how much wire you have left you should go around the actual ring part with the wire, not the decorative part but the part you actually put your finger in. Make sure you stay close to the top of the ring while you are wrapping the wire. Then you will trim the wire so that the cut end is on the outside of the ring, you want to make sure it is on the outside so it does not scratch your finger. Then just take your pliers and flatten that down. Do the same thing to the other side.

Once you have completed your ring place it back on the mandrel and just turn it on the mandrel what this will do is reshape the ring into a circle but it will also make sure the two wires are together.

If you want to add a little bit of bling to this ring one thing you can do is to add a few sparkly small beads to the wire as you are wrapping it close to the larger bead. It just gives a different look. You can also use three or four wraps around the mandrel to make the ring thicker. Each time you make this ring it will look different because each bead is unique and the wire will wrap differently each and every time. It is truly a one of a kind creation.

The last project we are going to work on is a pearl ring. But before we start the project I just wanted to drop in a few tips for you before the book ended. One of the best tips I ever got when I started making jewelry with beads was to order my beads online. When you go to a craft store and buy beads you will find that they are not all quality beads, some do not measure what the pack says they should, you can get seed beads that are not all the same size which can really mess up a project.

Another reason to purchase online is because of the cost. When I first started making beaded jewelry I was amazed at the price of beads but honestly if you look around online you can get them for 75 percent off of what you would pay at a craft store. So by ordering online you are getting better quality beads and paying less!

The next tip I have for you is to just relax and enjoy the learning process. I know a lot of people get into making jewelry because they want to sell it but you can tell if someone didn't enjoy making a project by the quality of the work so don't get upset if you get confused just relax and work through it.

The final tip I have for you is to make sure that you purchase an assortment of beads, clasps, wires, and chains for your projects as well as earring backs, chandeliers, and French wires. You never know which will be your favorite to work with so make sure you have several to choose from.
Now we can start our final project! The materials you will need for this project are 5g seed beads 11/0, 1 10mm round bead, 6 6mm round beads, 2 4mm round beads, about 1 yard of nylon thread .25mm.

The first step is to string 3 6mm round beads and pull them to the middle of the thread. (All black beads makes a beautiful ring) From this point you will want to work with the two ends of the thread, these will be the right thread and the left thread.

The next step is to sting 2 seed beads with the right thread and 2 seed beads with the left thread. Pick up the 10mm round bead and thread both threads through it each thread entering opposite sides of the bead. String two seed beads and one 6mm round bead through each of the threads separately. String one 6 mm round bead through both treads at the same time each thread entering opposite sides of the bead.

The next thing you want to do is string 10 seed beads on the right thread then pass through the 6mm round bead in the middle (there will be two pick one side to begin with) going from left to right. String 10 seed beads on the left thread and using the right thread pass through the 6 mm round bead in the middle going from right to left. Repeat this step for the opposite middle 6mm round bead.

With the right thread pass through the next 6mm round bead and do the same with the left thread. Now string 2 seed beads, one 4mm round bead and two more seed beads with the right thread, pass the thread thought the next 6mm round bead. Do the same thing with the left thread.

Cross both threads through the 6mm round bead in the middle. Now string three seed beads on each thread then pick up one seed bead and cross both threads through it entering from opposite sides. Repeat this until you have a strip almost the size that you want for the ring.

String three seed beads on each thread and cross thread them through the middle 6mm round bead on the opposite side making sure the strip goes under the cluster you have created.

With the right thread pass through the next 6 mm round bead and the next two seed beads, create a half knot. Pass through the next 4mm round bead and 2 seed beads, create another half knot. Pass through the next 6 mm round bead. Now do the same thing on the left side. After you have done this on the left side clip your threads and your ring is complete.

Did you know you can make your own beads? I am going to show you very quickly how to make your own beads. First you will need some glue, some newspaper and a plastic straw. Take your newspaper and lie it flat on the table, cut it about 2 inches shorter than the straw. Leaving one inch on each side of the straw, roll the newspaper around the straw.

As you are rolling brush glue on the paper so that it sticks together. Then slide the straw out of the paper. Cut off the ends of the newspaper roll so they are even then cut the newspaper to the size you want your beads to be. Reshape your beads by pitching them open and set them aside to dry.

Once the paper has dried you can use some acrylic paint to paint the ends any color you would like. Once the paint on the ends is dry you can finish up by painting the rest of the bead with varnish or clear nail polish. Then you can use your beads to make whatever you want. If you use newspaper with pictures instead of just words you will create some very interesting beads.

You can do this with any paper You can roll up printer paper and make small pictures on them before you coat them with clear nail polish, you can print out pictures, use magazine paper literally any type of paper. You can wrap the paper around different objects such as a paper clip to get different shapes as well.

Making your own beads is a great way for you to create unique pieces of art that no one will ever be able to copy.

Finally I want to finish up this book by teaching you how to make a bead ball, after you learn how to make a bead ball I will teach you how to use these bead balls to make a beautiful necklace or bracelet.

You will need three things to make your bead ball, first you will need your wire, this will give your bead ball a nice strong structure and it is very easy to work with although it is very difficult to create knots with. You will want to choose a thin but strong wire for the bead ball.

You can also use beading cord for this. Some people choose to use this because it is stronger than thread, and because it is clear. The problem with this is that it is very difficult to work with, and it does not create a strong structure.

You can also choose to used two needles, thread and a block of wax. Thread is very accessible but you do need wax to prevent it from breaking as you are working with it, thread does not give the ball any structure at all so you will need a center ball to keep the bead ball from caving in on itself.

For this project I will be discussing using wire but you can try all three, making three different balls and comparing them. You will need about 30 beads or crystals to start with. Cut one meter of wire and fold it in half so you can find the middle point. Thread five beads on to your wire, pushing them down to the middle of the wire. Straighten out where you bent the wire and take the end of your wire that is in your left hand and thread it through the last bead on the right hand side of the five you just threaded. This will form a loop. Thread three beads on the left wire and one bead on the right wire. Take your left wire and thread it through the bead you put on the right wire going in the opposite direction of the right wire. In other words you will insert the left wire into the hole the right wire is coming out of.

Tread your wire through the next bead as well, this will be the bead on the side of the loop you created previously. On the left wire, thread two beads, and with your right wire pick up one bead. Take your left wire and thread it through the bead you placed on the right wire going in the opposite direction of the right wire.

Then thread the left wire through the next bead just like you previously did. As you can see the beads are starting to take shape. Pick up two beads with your left wire and one bead with your right wire just like you did in the last step. Take your left wire and thread it through the one bead you put on your right wire going the opposite direction of the right wire.

Take the left wire and thread it through the next bead in the line as well. With your left wire pick up two beads and with your right wire pick up one bead, thread the left wire through the right bead and the next bead once again. You will close this off by threading through one more bead.

Pick up one bead on each side of your wire, take your left wire and thread it through the bead on the right. Take your left wire and thread it through the next bead. With your left wire you are going to pick up two beads, with your right wire you will pick up one bead and follow the same process as you did before.

Then take the right wire and thread it through the next two beads. Pick up one bead with your left wire and then thread it through the bead on the right wire going in the opposite direction of the right wire. And thread the left wire through the next two beads.

Thread one bead on each of your wires, take your left wire and thread it through the bead on the right going in the opposite direction of the right wire. Thread you left wire through the next two beads as well.

Pick up one bead on each wire, and at this point you should have one bead with, you are going to take your left wire and thread it through the one on the right. At this point you will have a perfect little ball but there will be a little gap. Take your left wire and thread it through the next three beads, now your wires should be opposite each other on the ball. Pick up your last bead with your left wire, thread your right wire back through it in the opposite direction of the left wire, pull the wires and you will have your finished ball.

Now you can either sting beads on the two sides of the necklace add a clasp and make a beautiful necklace out of this or you can tie off and save your bead for the necklace I am going to talk about next. It will be very difficult to tie the wire off so if you would prefer to make some with fishing line and a center bead just make sure you place your center bead in the ball when you get about half way through the bead ball. You also need to make sure that the bead you use for the center has a nice hole in it that you can use for stringing your necklace.

You can also make bracelets or even earrings out of these. I have seem people even add clusters of these bead balls onto headbands and hair clips.

For the necklace you are going to need about 40 of these bead balls depending on the size bead you choose to use, you will need illusion wire and a clasp. All you have to do is thread the illusion thread through the hole in the center bead in your bead balls. Tie your clasps on and your necklace is done. This is going to take a lot of work but once you create a few bead balls, they get much easier and you can create them in a matter of minutes.

This necklace is completely worth the time you are going to spend creating the bead balls and it is a fun necklace to make. You can also start with a center bead ball, add a few beads on each side of it and then another bead ball creating any pattern that you choose if you do not want to make 40 bead balls.

I hope you have enjoyed reading this book just as much as I have enjoyed writing it for you. I know there is a ton of information packed into this book but don't feel overwhelmed. Read through it a few times to make sure you absorb all of the information, work through each of these projects several times using different beads, different color wire and even thicker or thinner wire. Adjust all of these projects to fit your needs and your taste. There is nothing that says you have to make these projects exactly as I have stated. Just stick to the basics of the patterns and you and you can make anything you want.

Most of all enjoy the time you spend beading, you have taken this hobby up because you are creative and you love to make beautiful things. Don't allow the joy to be taken out of beading for you because you get stuck or do not understand something in this book. If you come across something that is unclear to you, take a step back and let your mind clear. When you come back to the project go back over the directions slowly and I can almost guarantee whatever you were having a problem with will click.

If you allow beading to frustrate you, you will lose the joy of creativity and you will eventually quit beading. Don't let this happen to you. Beading is a great way to reduce stress in your life if you do not allow it to cause more.

Happy beading to you and I sincerely hope this book has helped you learn how to bead and love it!

Conclusion

Thank you again for downloading this book!

Finally, if you enjoyed this book, please take the time to share your thoughts and post a review on Amazon. It'd be greatly appreciated!

Thank you and good luck!

Check Out My Other Books

Below you'll find some of my other popular books that are popular on Amazon and Kindle as well. Simply click on the links below to check them out. Alternatively, you can visit my author page on Amazon to see other work done by me.

- Handmade jewelry
- Puppy Training
- Explore the secrets of Machu Picchu
- Rome for travelers! The tourist´s guide to discover the capital of italy
- London for travelers : The tourist´s guide to discover the capital of uk
- Paris the city of love

If the links do not work, for whatever reason, you can simply search for these titles on the Amazon website to find them.

Jewerly :
Know all the gemstone and create your handmade jewelry empire

Table Of Contents

Copyright

Introduction

I want to thank you and congratulate you for downloading the book, Precious Stone Guide !

Know all the gemstone and create your handmade jewelry empire.

This book contains proven steps and strategies on how to use precious and semi-precious gemstones to build your beading empire.

In this book you are going to learn about the many different precious and semi-precious gemstones that you can use to create beaded jewelry as well as build your beaded jewelry business.

You will learn how what each gemstone looks like, where they originate, the different types of jewelry that can be made with each gemstone and so much more.

By the time you finish this book you will know everything you need to know in order to start using precious and semi-preciou gemstones in your beaded jewelry.

Thanks again for downloading this book, I hope you enjoy it!

Chapter 1

Agate to Azurite

Many people are making beaded jewelry and using it to earn an extra income but the mistake that they are making is that they are using plan cheap beads to create their jewelry. This causes the jewelry to look just as cheap as the beads are thus causing them to not sell.

People love handmade jewelry and they are willing to pay a good price to get it but they are not willing to pay for jewelry that looks like it was made by a child.

One thing that I have noticed is that people will purchase a bunch of cheap beads looking to make a quick profit but when that does not happen, they end up losing their investment.

Instead of purchasing cheap beads that no one is going to want jewelry made from, you need to consider purchasing some precious or semi-precious gemstone beads to make your jewelry.

These beads can be mixed with cheaper seed beads when making your jewelry but they should be used as a focal point in the jewelry.

In each chapter of this book we are going to learn about some of the precious and semi-precious beads that you can use in order to build your jewelry business.

Agate- This gemstone is available in many colors, including black, yellows, blue, browns, green, grey, white, pink, purple, read and orange. Typically this bead will have a beautiful pattern that resembles jasper but the colors are much more vivid. This gemstones markings will usually be in white but can come in an array of colors depending on the color of the bead. Yellow and green are less available than the other colors because they are so vivid and this is why they are the most sought after of all of the agate gemstones. Agate gemstones all so come in many different shapes and sizes so there is always one for any project that you are working on. Mix these with some seed beads of the same color and you will have a beautiful piece of jewelry.

2. Amazonite- This bead if often confused with turquoise because of its color, usually blue green to green. It can be mined in many place throughout the world but mostly in Australia. It is a great bead to use with fresh water pearls. You can use this bead for necklaces, bracelets or earrings and it makes a great focal point on rings.

3. Amber- One of my favorite beads, amber is created when sap from trees if fossilized. This takes many years to do and most of the amber that we find today is from prehistoric times. Amber comes in several shades of brown and is a clear bead. When heated in your hand amber is known to give off a pleasant scent. You can use amber in any of your jewelry and it will look elegant.

4. Amethyst- This bead is difficult for any beader as well as buyer to resist. The deep violet color makes jewelry stand out and the name means not drunk because it is believed that this bead helps protect the wearer from becoming drunk.

5. Green Amethyst- These beads were once only worn by royalty. The color is caused from heating pale lavender amethyst and although it is described as green the color is actually more clear with a slight tent of green. Today you can get these beads in any shape or size that you could ever want.

6. Ametrine- This does not often form in nature and what you will find today is generally replicated amethyst. As discussed previously when amethyst is heated it will turn different shades of yellow. In order to get the colors of ametrine the iron impurities have to be heated at different temperatures. This will result in several different colors.

7. Apatite- This bead has recently come onto the market and it known to have healing aspects. One of the many reasons people purchase beaded jewelry is because they believe specific gemstones possess different abilities such as healing

productivity and so on. This gemstone is believed to help with anxiety as well as eliminate stress.

8. Aquamarine- As its name suggest this is a beautiful blue gemstone that you can use when creating many different types of jewelry. It is a stone that many feel is very elegant and wear proudly. If you do not want to use this as your focal bead, the frosty appearance can be used to accentuate another bead. You could for example choose to create a necklace using aquamarine seed beads and use green amethyst as the focal beads. It is believed that this bead helps to soothe nerves and promote a feeling of peace.

9. Aventurine- This gemstone comes in several different colors including green, blue, yellow, orange, brown and gray. The stone is more opaque but can be translucent around the edges if light hits it. This is a quartz stone that contains small flecks which allows it to have a glistening effect. Depending on the size of the stone as well as the density you may see a lot of flecks or few.

Since the stone comes in such calming and relaxing colors it is believed that it helps rejuvenate a persons aura. It is also said to improve ones mood and help a person be more positive.

10. Azurite- Today this gemstone can be found in many beading supply stores and is usually a deep blue but is often found with green mixed in as well. This is because it is often found with Malachite both of which are formed from copper ore deposits. Many believe that this gemstone helps to activate the third eye or strengthen psychic abilities.

Chapter 2

Blue Opal- Coral

Some believe that because these precious and semi-precious gems are from the earth that they have different types of healing properties.

It is also believed that the shapes of the stones affect how they work as well so if this is an angle that you are planning on using when you are marketing your beaded jewelry you will need to take into consideration the types of stones you are using.

Another factor in the way the stone works is the color of the stone. You see many of these different gemstones will come in a variety of colors, sometimes the different colors will work in different ways. I do suggest that if you are going to use precious and semi-precious gemstones to make your beaded jewelry that you do use this technique when it comes to marketing.

It will expand your cliental and it will bring interest to your pieces by clients you may already have. It is believed that when you create jewelry with these precious and semi-precious gemstones that you are able to enhance the stones power by using precious metals and choosing the proper color stones.

This means that you can create jewelry to help with a specific health need as well as a specific spiritual need including specific blessings such as peace or prosperity. I have included in the book these spiritual meanings with many of the gemstones listed.

11. Blue Opal- Mostly found in Peru the blue opal does not represent the normal color of the opal gemstone. The problem with these beads is that because they are made from water and silica running through small cracks in the ground overtime, the bead is not wrapped in cotton and kept in a high humidity area it is likely to crack or break. The blue opal is the gemstone for Libra and signifies luck, prosperity, love and healing. It can be used in any number of handmade beaded jewelry project

and makes a great focal bead for rings. This gemstone is known as the gemstone of the gods and is said to be the strongest healing gemstone in the world.

12. Briolette- This bead is best used for necklaces or drop earrings because it is an elongated pear shape that is cut with facets and is often drilled to be a hanging bead. This bead was very popular during the Victorian times and it is currently seeing an increase in popularity once again. This gemstone comes in many different colors but the most popular of the Victorian time was the rose colored stone but today you can enjoy all of the wonderful colors. This stone is translucent and in India is described as the diamond. In fact, this tear drop shape was the original cut for most diamonds 800 years ago.

13. Cats Eye- It has been suggested that this bead will help to ensure the success in business of the owner and it is great for those who are starting a new business to wear. The bead is supposed to not only ensure that the wearer does not suffer loss but it is said to ensure the wearer is able to accumulate more. It is also said that this bead is great for anyone who is suffering from a skin disorder or allergies. The most popular and most expensive of all the cats eye beads is the chrysoberyl cat's eye. The reason it is called the cats eye is that it has a distinctive ability to reflect light in a slit in a way that resembles a cats eye. Some chrysoberyl have the ability to change color under light as well. This bead is usually round or oval shape so that when the light reflects off of it, it does resemble a cats eye and it is great to use in necklaces, earrings and even bracelets.

4. Chalcedony- Depending on how this term is used it can mean many different things, for example it can be used as a general term for all the different varieties of quartz that are made of submicroscopic or microscopic crystals. But a more strict definition would be fibrous grown crystals and the word is used to define a specific botryoidal specimen. Depending on what part of the world the chalcedony is from will determine what it looks like and what colors are available. For example if it is from Mexico it may look like a rainbow of colors but if it is from New Mexico it is as white as a pearl. You want to make sure that if

you are planning on using this gemstone that you pay attention to where it is from or the color that you are ordering so you do not become disappointed when you get your beads. It is said that this stone can help expel evil spirits and help anyone who is suffering from nightmares. In the middle ages, astrologers would make magic stones out of this gemstone by carving signet rings in them. The Burmese tribe kept these stone in their houses to protect their families and even sailors wore them to protect them from drowning.

15. Charoite- This gemstone is very rare and it is only found in Russia, the weather is so severe and the ground too dangerous to drive which causes miners to only be able to get to the area where this gemstone is located by helicopter. The name of the stone originated with the Russian word chary which when translated means magic. The stone is usually full of swirls of different colors and often consist of Tinkasite. The Charoite is known as a soul stone which brings healing to the body as well as the emotions. It is said that this stone will help the wearer to overcome addictions, as well as gives energy to an exhausted body. It is also said that this stone helps to regulate blood pressure and help the wearer sleep well and experience powerful dreams.

16. Chrysocolla- This bead is also said to help boost energy for the wearer and many Native American tribes considered it a stone that had the ability to heal and bring calmness to a wearer that was feeling extremely stressed out. It is said to encourage levelheadedness and allow the wearer to remain calm and collected when faced with a chaotic situation. It is also said that this stone can help reduce anger as well as anxiety. The stone is also known for its feminine powers and helps the wearer to express gentleness. Chrysolcolla is a copper carbonate and comes in a gorgeous blue color. It is often confused with turquoise because both stones share many visual qualities and is great to intermingle with turquoise when creating beaded jewelry because it creates an interesting visual affect. Since the stone is a soft stone it is often coated with a clear coating to make it more durable. Household cleaners as well as excessive heat should be kept away from this stone.

17. Chrysoprase- Or the Stone of Venus, is a very rich apple green stone that was mistake for emerald by early jewelers. But unlike emerald, Chryoprase contains trace amounts of nickel instead of receiving its color from chromium. Even though the apple green is the most popular color of Chryoprase, it does come in much darker greens as well as much lighter greens. It is said to help bring the unconscious into the conscious world, meaning that it helps bring those unconscious desires into reality. It is also known as a gemstone that helps to clarify the mind and allow the wearer to overcome problems. This gemstone has also been used to help those who suffer from restlessness as well as a stone of protection for those going off to voyage at sea.

18. Citrine- This stone is a member of the quartz family and is a translucent yellow-gold color. This gemstone is very affordable but is very durable as well so it is great for making beaded jewelry out of. The stone comes in many shapes and sizes as well as many different cuts allowing for different affects when light hits the stone. It looks very elegant and should be used as a focal bead. It can be used to create any number of different pieces of beaded jewelry and looks best when mixed with other translucent beads. This bead has also been referred to as the stone of the mind, and in many early cultures this stone was worn around the forehead of the elders because it was believed to help them think more clearly and to boost psychic powers. This stone is also known as a merchant stone which means that it helps those who are in sales. It is said that if you wear this stone and you are in sales, you can watch your money increase daily.

19. Conch Shell- This bead is named after the people of Burma and these beads have been used for several centuries. They come in a beautiful pink as well as off white colors and many different shapes and sizes. This bead can be used as a focal bead but I think it is best used as an accent. It is believed that the conch shell beads help to drive out evil spirits as well as help the wearer avert disaster.

20. Coral Beads- This stone is very valuable and is available in dark brilliant colors as well as lighter colors. These are usually dark

read to a light pink. These beads are made out of actual coral which is a calcium carbonite that is combined with magnesium as well as some organic substance. This bead is believed to help the wearer overcome specific diseases such as chicken pox, disease of the blood, impotency, chronic pain and excessive tiredness. It is also used to bring peace into a marriage.

Chapter 3
Crystal- Jasper

You can choose to get smooth beads which have been tumbled to make them look the way they do but you should also consider getting the gemstone in the rough. These stones are in their natural state and make a great focal point for necklaces as well as bracelets.

The stones in their natural state come in various shapes and sizes which means that you may have to search a little bit for the perfect stone but your customers will love it. You could also consider wrapping these stones in wire to give it a more finished look and to ensure you do not have to drill a hole into the stones.

1. Crystal- These beads come in a variety of different colors and these are what colored glass beads are usually made to look like. Some of these beads are completely translucent but there are others that almost look as if a cloud is captured in the gemstone. Real crystal beads come in many shapes and sizes but generally they are odd shapes. They are not perfectly cut unlike their glass bead counterparts. It is believed that these beads can have a huge effect on the wearers emotional, physical, spiritual and mental well-being. This gemstone is used in healing ceremonies as well as used for protection from supernatural entities. The amazing thing about this gemstone is that it does not matter what the size of the stone is, they all have the same ability to heal the wearer.

2. Druzy- This gemstone is actually a cluster of tiny gemstones that has occurred on the surface of a rock. Druzy has a very sparkly appearance and for this reason it is used in jewelry. I comes in a variety of colors as well as shapes. This is a great gemstone to use as a focal point for rings. This stone is said to help motivate the wearer as well as enhance the abilities of the stone that it is paired with thus making it a great stone to use with other gemstones of like colors.

23. Emerald- This is a gemstone that many of us already know about, it is a beautiful green and is usually associated with Ireland but the name of the stone actually originated from the French word, esmeraude which literally means green stone. It is believed that this stone promotes love and success in relationships and it is said that if the color of the emerald that is being worn changes even slightly it is a sign of unfaithfulness. This stone also is said to help bring balance into the wearers entire life.

24. Feldspar- The name feldspar actually describes an entire group of gemstones because there are several different crystals that fall under this name but the specific beads I want to talk about are referred to simply as golden feldspar because they have yet to be given a name. This is a translucent bead which comes in many different shapes and cuts. It is a very popular gemstone and is said to help eliminate the feeling of misery in the wearer. It is also said to help those who are suffering from guilt. Many people believe that by wearing this stone they are able to look at the world from a more positive perspective and that it helps remove negative feelings from their life.

25. Florite- This is a translucent gemstone that comes in a rainbow of colors, it is a very popular bead because it has several different colors in one bead. This is one of the gemstones that looks very beautiful in its natural state as well as when it has been finished to so it gives you many more options when you are creating jewelry. Egyptians used to use Florite to carve statues and other figurines and it has even been used to treat kidney disease by crushing it and placing it in water. It is said that this gemstone has the ability to reduce negativity in ones life, help with concentration as well as increases ones learning ability, improves balance in the wearers life, increases the immune system of the wearer, helps with skin conditions, as well chronic pain. This bead can be used as a focal bead or it can be used throughout an entire piece of jewelry or with other gemstones.

26. Garnet- This is another crystal gemstone that comes in a variety of colors but the most well-known color of this gemstone is the

deep red. These gemstones were often used in the Roman Empire and the blue garnet is the rarest color. This gem stone comes in many different shapes and sizes as well as cuts like many of the other gemstones so it can be used in many different pieces of jewelry. This is a very elegant stone and it should be used only as a focal bead because using too much garnet in one piece will take away from its beauty. It is said that this gemstone will help to increase your energy levels as well as the endurance of the wearer. This gemstone is also known for increasing the success of the wearer when it comes to business ventures and money. This stone is recognized as a high class stone and is mostly worn by women.

27. Howlite- This gemstone is also known as the white buffalo stone, because of its white color. The gemstone also has grey veins running through it, but most of the time you will not find the gemstone in this state because it is so often dyed other colors such as blue, green, or red. The reason that this gemstone is dyed is so that it is able to resemble more expensive gemstones. If you are going to use this gemstone I suggest that you look for it in its natural color because it is very attractive. This stone is said to help the wearer to obtain the power of knowledge and it is said to help rid the wearer of anxiety. Many believe that this gemstone will help the wearer begin to understand how their actions will affect other areas of their lives or other people in their life. It is also said that this gemstone helps the wearer work through any issues that they have suffered from in this life as well as past lives.

28. Ironstone- This gemstone is created out of sediment and usually has a large amount of iron in it which is what gives it its name as well as the weight of the stone. This stone should be used as a focal point bead because of the weight you would not want to create an entire necklace or bracelet out of it. It is not recommended to be used in drop earrings because it is so heavy. The gemstone is usually found with a brown color due to the oxidization of the iron but when it is finished the stone can be black or red and banded which is why many refer to it as the tiger iron stone. It is believed that this stone helps to increase energy as well as confidence in the wearer and that it helps the

wearer to overcome mental or emotional issues that they have been dealing with. The stone is also said to help increase creativity in the wearer as well as aid in the absorption of Iron and vitamin B.

29. Ivoryite- This gemstone gets its name because it is very white and looks a lot like ivory but the gemstone is very fragile and care must be taken not to break the stone. This gemstone is usually very small and should be used to accent another gemstone. This gemstone is known for helping the wearer keep a level head when they are facing a lot of pressure in different areas of their life and works best when paired with another gemstone that focuses on specific areas.

30. Jade- This is another gemstone that many of us are familiar with but may not really know a lot about. Jade comes in the color green but may come in many different shades. Some jade may be translucent while others are more opaque. The Chinese believe that this stone will draw out hidden love and they are often used to represent love. This stone is also believed to help with prosperity and attract money into your life. It allows the wearer to have a more positive outlook on money and helps them to use the money they have more wisely. Many people believe that if you hold the bead in your hand and imagine yourself spending money wisely and not on frivolous purchase, that the gemstone will help to make this happen in your life.

31. Jasper- This stone comes in many different colors including brown, yellow, green, red, white, blue and more. The gemston can be a solid color but more likely it will be spotted or hav some natural design on it. This gemstone that is even mentione in the Bible, and it is usually a very inexpensive and is quit common today. The gemstone is usually used for beaded jewelr projects such as earrings, bracelets and necklaces. I would no suggest that this bead be used as a focal bead on a ring unles you find a very special and beautiful bead. It is believed tha Jasper brings power to the life of the wearer and that since it an Earth stone it also helps to ground the wearer. Jasper is als known for bringing stability into ones life, and helping to defen the wearer against anything that would come against the.

Chapter 4
Kyanite-Mammoth

When you are beading it is very important to pay attention to the color of the gemstones. Remember that just because two gemstones look nice apart it does not mean they will look nice together. For example if you are using jade to bead with you would want to complement this with another green gemstone, a white or even a black gemstone. What you would not want to do is to create an odd mixture of different colored gemstones just because you feel someone else my like it. Focus on elegance and you will have no problem creating beautiful beaded jewelry.

In the final chapter of this book, I want to go over a few more gemstones. I wish that I could cover every gemstone in the world but that is simply not possible. I do however want to make sure you get as much information as I can provide you with on each of the gemstones listed in this book.

32. Kyanite- The name of this gemstone came from the Greek word kyanos which means deep blue. This stone does come in a deep blue color but it also has a variety of blue colors to choose from many of them accented with white in the stone. It has been used to track the Earths magnetic pull by travelers allowing them to tell where North is. Kyanite is also available in orange and the variation of the gemstone was found in Tanzania the blue colored stone can be found all over the world in places that include the USA, Brazil and Kenya. Kyanite is said to help clear negative energies from the wearers life as well as correct internal imbalances.

33. Lapis- The Lapis gemstone is an ancient gemstone that was used in Egyptian traditions. The Egyptians put the gemstone in the tombs of the pharaohs because it was believed that the gemstone would provide protection from the tombs being looted. Many early cultures valued lapis more than they valued gold and even believed that it could predict if their partner would be unfaithful to them. It is also believed that you must be very careful when working with this gemstone because it can open you up

becoming a channel for the other side and even give you psychic abilities. Lapis is believed to be a representation of the truth.

34. Lava- Not so much a precious gemstone as one that is not seen as often in jewelry this gemstone can really set your beading business apart from the rest. It is said that you should wear lava beads in a time of change to ensure that the changes that occur are permanent. Of course you would not want to do this if the changes are not ones that please you. This bead is also though to help the wearer connect with the Earth, grounding them as well as brining balance into their life. These beads are from natural flowing lava which means that no matter how each one is shaped, they are all unique into themselves.

35. Mammoth- These beads are quite distinctive in color and often look like an old bone. These are usually tens of thousands of years old and although rare are a great find for a beader. Since the gemstone is only found in areas such as Alaska, Canada and Siberia it can only be mined a few months out of each year when the summer thaw happens. Since the Mammoths died out so long ago this gemstone is very rare as well as very expensive and most scientists would not be happy to have it sold on a piece of jewelry but since it does not endanger any animals there is nothing that can be done about beaders using it. This stone is also known as mammoth rock.

Those are all of the gemstones I have space to cover in this book but don't forget that there is an entire world out there full of gemstones, precious and semi-precious for you to use in all of your beaded jewelry creations.

I hope that through this book you have been able to understand a little bit more about precious and semi-precious gemstones so that you can use them to build your beading empire. I also hope that you have enjoyed reading this book and learning all of this information as much as I enjoyed writing it for you.